Music Minus One Piano

6016

Wolfgang Amadeus MOZART

PIANO CONCERTO No. 1
IN F MAJOR, KV37

PIANO CONCERTO No. 3
IN D MAJOR, KV40

Suggestions for using this MMO edition

WE HAVE TRIED to create a product that will provide you an easy way to learn and perform these concerti with a full orchestra in the comfort of your own home. Because it involves a fixed orchestral performance, there is an inherent lack of flexibility in tempo and cadenza length. The following MMO features and techniques will reduce these inflexibilities and help you maximize the effectiveness of the MMO practice and performance system:

Where the soloist begins a movement *solo*, we have provided an introductory measure with subtle taps inserted at the actual tempo before the soloist's entrance. We have also added subtle taps in the accompaniment version recording where a sudden tempo change or ambiguous accompaniment line demands them.

Chapter stops on your CD are conveniently located throughout the piece at the beginnings of practice sections, and are cross-referenced in the score. This should help you quickly find a desired place in the music as you learn the piece.

Chapter stops have also been placed at orchestra entrances (e.g., after cadenzas) so that, with the help of a second person, it is possible to perform a seamless version of the concerto alongside your MMO CD accompaniment. While we have allotted what is generally considered an average amount of time for a cadenza, each performer will have a different interpretation and observe individual tempi. Your personal rendition may preclude a perfect "fit" within the space provided. Therefore, by having a second person press the pause❙❙button on your CD player after the start of each cadenza, followed by the next track▶▶❙button, your CD will be cued to the orchestra's re-entry. When you as soloist are at the end of the cadenza or other solo passage, the second person can press the play▶(or pause❙❙button) on the CD remote to allow a synchronized orchestra re-entry.

We have observed generally accepted tempi, but some may wish to perform at a different tempo, or to slow down or speed up the accompaniment for practice purposes. You can purchase from MMO (or from other audio and electronics dealers) specialized CD players & recorders which allow variable speed while maintaining proper pitch. This is an indispensable tool for the serious musician and you may wish to look into purchasing this useful piece of equipment for full enjoyment of all your MMO editions.

We want to provide you with the most useful practice and performance accompaniments possible. If you have any suggestions for improving the MMO system, please feel free to contact us. You can reach us by e-mail at info@musicminusone.com.

A note about the 'practice tempo' disc

As an aid during the early stages of learning these concerti, we have created a second 'practice tempo' compact disc which is identical to the main performance and practice disc in layout, but for which the 'minus' version has been slowed by approximately 12.5%. This will allow you to begin at a comfortably reduced speed until fingerings and technique are more firmly in grasp, at which time the full-speed disc can be substituted. Please note that due to the digital handiwork required to slow the tempo, you may notice a slight degradation of sound quality in these reduced-tempo practice accompaniments on the 'B' disc.

Music Minus One

MMO
6016

Wolfgang Amadeus MOZART

CONCERTO № 1
in F MAJOR
for PIANO *and* ORCHESTRA
KV37

CONCERTO № 3
in D MAJOR
for PIANO *and* ORCHESTRA
KV40

MMO 6016

Wolfgang Amadeus
MOZART

CONCERTO
№ 1

in

F MAJOR

for

PIANO

and

ORCHESTRA

KV37

MMO 6016

CONCERTO Nº 1
in D MAJOR
for
PIANO *and* ORCHESTRA
KV37

Wolfgang Amadeus Mozart
(1756-1791)

MMO 6016

* Originaly with trill

II

* Originaly c sharp

Cadenza

III

Wolfgang Amadeus
MOZART

CONCERTO
№ 3

in

D MAJOR

for

PIANO

and

ORCHESTRA

KV40

MMO 6016

CONCERTO № 3
in D MAJOR
for
PIANO and ORCHESTRA
KV40

Wolfgang Amadeus Mozart
(1756-1791)

Corni

dolce

Cadenza

II

III

*) Seconda volta

Engraving: Wieslaw Novak

MMO 6016

MUSIC MINUS ONE
50 Executive Boulevard
Elmsford, New York 10523-1325
800-669-7464 (U.S.)/914-592-1188 (International)

www.musicminusone.com
e-mail: mmogroup@musicminusone.com

Printed in Canada